Poet Eight Vagabond Poet Eig

night exposures

by

Gerry Loose

Vagabond Voices
Glasgow

© Gerry Loose 2018

First published on 14 June 2018 by
Vagabond Voices Publishing Ltd.,
Glasgow,
Scotland.

ISBN 978-1-908251-94-7

The author's right to be identified as author of this book under the Copyright, Designs and Patents Act 1988 has been asserted.

Printed and bound in Poland

Cover design by Mark Mechan

Typeset by Park Productions

The publisher acknowledges subsidy towards this publication from Creative Scotland

ALBA | CHRUTHACHAIL

For further information on Vagabond Voices, see the website, www.vagabondvoices.co.uk

Contents

five cantations for endangered species	3
night exposures	7
Island Stories	41
A Brief Incomplete History of Nuremberg	47
Sweeney Albannach	63
on being in a place / on being in place	95
Acknowledgements	109

ps
night exposures

five cantations for endangered species

syllable seeds for the
bardo of vascular plants

for the chaff the bog
wood-small narrow-small
for dense-flowered the small-flowered
for few-flowered the green-flowered
soft melancholy
purple ramping
meadow-bed
wood-field
heath-holy
for the water the smooth
for the lesser the cloud
for the great the annual
fen and marsh
tresses and cress

thus

instar for the bardo of coleoptera

dive rove crawl hop chafe
quicksilver copper bronze
bereft transition

an offering

syllables for the bardo of bryophytes

pass ribbed
pass earth
pass feather
pass slender
pass rigid
pass dwarf
pass fat bud
pass thread
pass hook
pass stook
horn pouch pinch
notch frost rust

pass

chrysalis for the bardo of lepidoptera

dagger with knot
forester with pinion
chestnut with crescent
mouse with tiger
dusky with sallow
sprawler with shoulder
mottled with streak
latticed with brindled
grey with yellow
double with narrow
ghost with plume
crimson & gold
argent & sable
cinnabar & red
neglected sword

so be it

**liminal
bardo of hymenoptera**

shiny margined
short horned
small flecked
grey banded
yellow faced
dark winged
blunt jawed
dull headed
solitary
cuckoo
nomad
blood

be

night exposures

walking on
dry gravel
bed running
between trees

***

she drowns in the canal
beside a towpath
at a lock

behind on the towpath
2 women
discuss a court
appearance

***

the journey
the fleeting moment

while she sleeps
someone falls in the water

while he sleeps
little girl falls in the water

the same time

***

given up everything
penniless

they   *all strangers*

geologists
earthmoving
machines at workings

listen to the explan-
ation of sandstorms
horizons obscured

lean back

eyes shut
wire fence

tell of
a soldier
stroking his beard
but also of
his shaking hands

***

loss

***

Pabum. *No.*
pabulum

***

public political speech
men in shades
among crowd giving
random beatings

leaders talking
thanking each other

fathers at war
mothers giving birth

***

constraints

sexual nature

someone is there

who is wandering

around there?

***

little low hills
given over to wheat

***

(   )

***

the sky
knows

speedwell
forget-me-not

***

she becomes aroused
the house is full

***

his calves
seen through
(a tear)
curtaining
waves

leaves' pattern

***

old houses bulging at the back

touch across the little alley

a new wrought railing

angry about children

squinting in the sun

domestic matters

***

caravan deep into wilderness
is mother is father

watch orchestrated ball games
in an orchard there

the crabs have withered apples
prepare for winter

***

tending two fires
in cottage

to keep folk warm
the battered ash

***

's a being (of that world)
large   substantial
human   woman

with other humans women
waiting for their interpreter
dressed (as they're naked)

face each other
in a small circle
silent   waiting

***

use creosote

two old friends
just met

pinholes in the pages
show a constellation

of light

***

stag   stab

there are three
one with stag horns

along a deep lane
to a dead end
he is transfixed
with sharp antlers
an axe thumps
into his throat
scramble the bank
escape
here now

***

(   )

***

all's well

a nonsense

***

a son's with

*

unpaved road
along cliff edge

across dry sandy
arroyos where
rivers once fell
cliff edge
waterfalls

***

playing small
stringed instrument

***

giant wild puck

goat   horns
larger than ever seen

grab horns under
oxter   drag

home
horns

come off

***

searching for Pretty Boy
who's not found

but the stillness after

& shock of finding

of which
no knowledge

*recognise people
other than*

***

part of resistance
to occupying army

disguise theft
of their cement

render it smooth
to delay them

sharpen knives

***

something menacing
rising

&
above a wall

a wall

*

on juggernauts
(child refugees
running in front/alongside

along canals
under rains

water swilling
around seats)
a political meeting

tending
demonstrating
winter tree pruning

a suspended
pollarded living tree
no roots

***

another wall

another rising

again

went to grandma's

up a ramshackle

ladder

***

small things
domestic things

asking for groceries
on credit

***

memory
hides

is broken
with steel

deceiving
edges

***

taking
pills
made
of
iron

***

deep in
trees trunks

stems boles
nothing else

***

cooking on a
black iron stove

under a tree
no fuel

estranged daughter
begins to talk

***

are pointed

diving
deep

nothing
there

***

instead of tongue as
tongue leaf

**

the little bird sings
the little dog laughs
the last bird
the last dog
the last laugh
they were lonely
the third bell
the seventh bell
the ninth bell
the last planet

***

the list of
things
re/member

**

they are executing him
automatic weapons

others dance
in a circle slowly

***

old woman's
released from

darkness
fed

***

new moon
vixen calling

calling

***

( ) religious ceremony
( ) transmission

all are naked

after
fruit & blossoms're lying

on grass beside
the path

***

journeying
along a canal for

ceremonial purpose
handfuls

objects mirrors handles
empty cloth bags

journeying
along single track

roads   escaping
oil changing

bleeding aircraft
brakes leaking

at stand
still

***

the architect drives
( ) to his room

the baby is dropped
knows only kindness

***

swarming
Milky Way

dog fox
barking

***

inventing
numerical table

mirror image
pair of triangles

adjoined at base
with perfectly

reflecting
different numbers

up & down
the scale

***

butcher in apron
wind running

someone
stolen

heavy eyelids fluttering
opening

***

visiting a gangster
songs are good

emergency exit

**

in greaseproof
blisterpacked

tablets   smoke
inhaled from

inches away no need
to suck the end

***

can't find the
two smallest children

***

planting
restricted

cuneate
unrevealed

***

canal of mud
flowing along the street

little is lost
at the edge

***

smiling mouth

stabs an eye

***

mother's

alive

baby

's getting

fat

***

walking in
back alleys

city's
night

rooftop aviaries
women

singing

***

waiting for a bus
all that's owned

waiting for the verdict
court of religion

never make it
it's not there

heron's gone

river in flood

***

's swelling
telling

a story

***

triangular space
high wooden

walls
secrets

***

parrot is
singing with a

human voice
after all

***

we are being

someone else

***

for part of the route
there's only photographs

***

moths devouring
each other

Snake
Monkey sit in

glowing coals
She appears

things go awry
Chorus

***

the acqueduct-bridge
closed to humans

's to be painted
sky blue with water

fade
against sky

***

she brought a
green pumpkin

***

plottings. plans.
assassination.

***

in cottage
short sweet lyrics

century third
open window bird

song

realise not enough
time

is called

***

hold the new
born baby

for the first
time

***

pissing a
long time
a hole in

chemical crust
ground dirty
polluted

the dog is lost
that spoke

're in the mountains
on steep
boulder strewn trails
between villages
pack animals
black
bony

***

on the way back
the public vehicle stops
small coastal village
river meets sea
fish market
front for the guns

bid a man good morning
in the afternoon

***

defend
death

paint a picture in
quick brushstrokes

a mushroom cloud
souvenir

***

go absent walking more
than once
watching life

***

hiding in caves
at the end of the
island
invaders
murderer-raiders
come

*

cops
make us sign
to park

*

mockfucking
in the house
she says
we have the sunlight

***

he wants to kill
run
along canal banks
through shopping malls
climb walls

(the rich live here
now)

***

nimbus of flying insects

small boy talking

Dalai Lama visits

***

climbing wild
mountain
's green red scree
lone trees bare
two men in the
cave on small motor
bikes not /asking
for bribes
trying to hide the old rifle
no trigger

shanties where we
will wait for
bandit-inspectors

***

shelter in
tiny pavilion
pull it
back
like a kite

***

arrested by
unshaven sheriff

hands cuffed
behind back

driven off

no papers
(   )

other cop
casually beating

not
being silent

***

taken hostage

*

where houses
stop
cliff's edge
a small bridge
to an island

***

leaving.

disagreements

with a sister

***

no
sleekness
of *before*

***

blessing
from

who instructs
on procedure

Island Stories

At the philosopher's house the spices are in two drawers, in jars on their sides, labels up. They are arranged alphabetically. The last, newly bought, is za'atar. Each day a hare sits on the grass beside the philosopher's veranda.

The gardener does not hear time. She listens to aspens which are tremulous in wind. She listens to the wing-swish of swallows and the chitter of their voices. She hears distant greylags clearing long throats to ululate. The last light is falling, or darkness is rising.

The mushroom hunter would tie a little bell to her basket to let bears know she was in the forest. Her house among the trees burned down. How hard it is to push her chair, she who danced, she who danced and flew. Her eyes are the salt of the Baltic sea.

The new old man is a younger woman. Her name is noble, is a fairy story. She pruned trees. She planted trees. Her language is a poetry of saws, leaned shovels, blue-handled rakes. She does not wear a seat belt when she drives her white van. She stores useful timber. There is an axe in the sauna.

One on the island does nothing all day. In the morning he says goodbye to a friend who is leaving for the capital. In the afternoon he collects birch bark, strips it and cuts it into two inch squares. He writes on these squares.

The stonemason is beachcombing in the forest. Constant wind in the forest canopy is an ocean. He never knows what might turn up here. Today he has found four colours. Sulphur yellow of lichen on a birch trunk. Lemon yellow of six aspen leaves, each with a lime-green leaf gall. A small toothed crimson leaf. He carries colour to the hut in the forest.

The postman has no letters to deliver today. He smokes a cigarette. The raspberries are ripe. His eyesight is getting worse. No junk mail, no State missives. He thinks of perch for supper. The hour thickens. He smokes another cigarette.

With evening a little wind dances. The vodka drinker sits on a smoothed boulder. He steals glances to left and right, drinks from the glass in his left hand. Take not so much as a pin that's not yours, he remembers his mother saying. An adder comes and goes. He admires the geese flying west to east. To the east he thinks. Vodka freezes at minus 26.95 degrees he says, quietly, to himself.

A Jewish boy in wartime was sent to the farm where food was eaten from the boards of the table. In his dream the gourmand is served with delicacies by the chef directly onto the table. The proprietor chef urges him to eat faster and sweeps all the tiny delicacies onto a plate. Mixed in is a bloodied bandage from a finger. The gourmand wakes, thinking for some time that he is a butterfly.

The one who does nothing weaves his bike along the dirt road in order not to ride onto grasshoppers and caterpillars. There are beetles crossing too. In his basket is a loaf of island bread, just bought. He would like to share it with someone. A dog maybe. Or a hare. After de Nerval walked his pet lobster on that blue silk lead, did he feed it bread?

The new old man, who is a younger woman, is picking berries. Raspberries, red and black currants. It's part of her job. The vodka drinker is walking by and stops; picks a few raspberries too, which he eats. He takes a flat plastic bottle from his jacket pocket. It has a picture of an elk on the label. Vodka. He unscrews the cap, offers it to the new old man. She shakes her head; a small tightening of the lips. The vodka drinker stares at the younger woman and sips delicately from the neck of the bottle.

The gardener hears and listens to the booms of thunder from the approaching storm. The way the world speaks to us. Today, reluctantly, she accepts an official letter from the postman. Speak softly to the world she says to him.

Last night, as light rose from the grasses, the hare

visited again. The philosopher cannot realise his equation. He disgusts himself. He would like not to think. The forest trees grow straight. He has an oiled Luger pistol in his desk drawer.

Bell silenced, there will be no bears today. Eyes and ears tuned to the forest, the mushroom hunter hears the stonemason before she sees him. She remains motionless behind an old birch trunk. She is ashamed of her lack of generosity. She grips her knife tightly.

The gourmand likes the empty red barns and their sagging doors. They are not spaces to be filled. They are already full of dreams of cows for the suck of calves. Of dreams of wheat and of oats to seed the land in tides and surfs of inland seas. His blue eyes are terrible and lit with the sad compassion of those who are intimate with death. His slow hand flicks the porch light on and he enters his house.

The apples are not ripe yet. The stonemason knows that, without twisting one on its stem, but cannot resist. As a child, he'd believed the apples were red because of the communist executed against the twisted pine tree off to one side of the old orchard.

Now there's only us, the postman is saying, but maybe to himself. Us and the summer houses. They only see the forest and complain of mosquitoes, get drunk. They can't see our memories: the rock we dived from. Where we picked berries. My first lovemaking in the moss. She was my love the whole summer. Without our memories this is just a place. And bitter. Maybe better that way.

The philosopher stands at the open window and watches the rain. It's that day again in 1918 on the island. His father's story of grandfather. That day in 1936. His memories sicken him. The ammunition is in the drawer below the Luger.

The one who does nothing comes across the gourmand in the heart of the forest collecting mushrooms. Eying the gourmand's knife, the one asks for advice. The gourmand looks at him for a long time. Finally he says: always wash your hands after chopping chillies.

The postman speaks circumspectly about the philosopher's hare. He lights a cigarette.

The philosopher decides against picking mushrooms. They are like an equation that doesn't balance. There is no fire in his equation. A dead damselfly in the bathroom crystallises his thought. Like that, he says. Ex nihilio nihil fit. Nothing comes from nothing.

The vodka drinker has his back to a pine at the edge of the forest by the sea. He is always at the edge of drunkenness, but never reaches it, being intoxicated instead. He is not given to reminiscence; his mind is like a series of drawers containing spices, string, a pistol, but that one is swollen shut.

The new old man, a young woman, falters outside the front door.

Not for the first time he is woken by the roaring sound of blood coursing through his body. A sound he wants to stop. He lifts his head from the pillow.

Her sadness grows and fills the room, pressing into each corner across the ceiling.

He softly sings a snatch of an aria from Julius Caesar: *Shine on, forever shine in grace and beauty.*

The pistol lies between them.

On the island there is a glazier and a funeral director. They are the same person. His vision is clear, unimpaired.

A Brief Incomplete History of Nuremberg

The sun is radiant this morning. Agathe Paul forgets how to say Middle East. She struggles and tries Near East, turns to me and asks – Sir, is this correct? She asks what comes to mind when I think of Nuremberg. Although I have been thinking of Dürer, she suggests the Nuremberg Trials. In the shop window, Dürer's hare is a fine shade of purple.

**

Katharina is almost three years old. In the garden the old bench is near collapse. Katharina has her hands clasped behind her back. Oh no! she says. And again. Oh no!

**

The Flesh Bridge between St Sebald and St Lorenz tells me: All things have a beginning and grow, but the ox upon whom you now look was never a calf.

**

On the Saturday Herr Wolf the butcher gives each of his customers a single red rose. This is to celebrate Mothering Sunday, when he is closed. His old father collects wild garlic every spring which Herr Wolf makes into a relish. Once, we lived in the countryside, he says.

**

It's the first garden get-together of the year for old friends. There is a crate of beer and a bonfire. Arno tends the fire with a new stainless steel long-handled spade. In the rising heat the newly leafed maple branches are swaying, coasting like a thousand bird wings. Michael will not leave until the fire is nothing but embers, safe. He was once a volunteer firefighter. Now he lives in a city-wall tower. The roof beams there are wooden, massive and exposed.

***

Max tells me ninety-eight per cent of wine is shit. He is unequivocal. It's a description he enjoys. He relishes the word, rolls it in his mouth even as I savour his champagne: his real naked champagne he tells me, zero dressage, pure Chardonnay, four years on lees in the bottle. Shit! he carefully articulates, once again. Max is not prosaic; his speech is grape-lyric, an ancient thing, clustered with the old vines of dusty hillsides. Passion. Here we used to drink lean, meagre and sour wines he says. No longer. Wine doesn't taste, wine gives a feeling. This – he gestures at his Larmandier-Bernier – has finesse, freshness, elegance. It is not able to be manipulated. We drink on. The taste of wine is just conventional; the secret for wine is the word; how it must be discussed and described. It is communication with yourself. Another gesture for a Mosel River Riesling: the lees is saying I can't ferment your sugar any more; I'm done. The Crianza has been two years in the bottle – Max is speaking fast – the Australians put sex, drugs and rock and roll in the glass. Europe has redefined its definition of what organic means. Forty-five of forty-eight inorganic additions to wine are now classified as organic. Ho. Ho. he says, very slowly. Another fling of the arm: here we have brioche, hazelnuts, brown butter. I have long since forgotten what we are drinking. Max is spectacular. He stares at me. I stare back. He speaks sadly: All this kind of shit has no relation to reality. Wine is communication.

**

Agnieszka arrived from Poland at the age of 16. She lodged with the nuns. At night, at lights out after prayers, she had to keep both hands above the blanket, flat, in clear view.

**

Can you tell me where Albrecht Dürer's grave is, she asks. I've lived in Nuremberg since I was born and I've never visited his grave.
Joachim von Sandrart, lying there more than four hundred years, lives to die, dies to live. Der du bist, der war ich. How many of us there are here. Anni Gerl, at ninety seven and just laid down, smiles. She is still hungry. She remembers those years. Hungry for life, hungry for rest. We walk to the grave together. There is a clump of shepherd's purse at its foot. It will rain.

**

Lumen de lumine:1698 and he still recalls the sun streaming through the plane trees by the river along Hallerwiese at noon, St Sebaldus' bells ringing clear in the distance. It resembles Charpentier's Midnight Mass. Light from light.

**

The hangman's hand is still intact, severed, under the axe, by Henkersteg near the wine store and the mature willow.

**

Carlos the Cultural Director says we're trying to use culture to revitalise communities. What Kristian the Creative Communicator-Coordinator does not say is when Capitalism bankrupts itself it turns to artists.

**

When Arnold was ten years old he met Hermann Kesten at a reading. Shy and naive, he was the first to ask a question: Your name is Kesten; did you know Kessler? To which Kesten replied, yes; he is a friend. The ten-year-old and Kesten corresponded for many years. Arnold explains his work: the Nazis are only a pale frame. We must also deal with other types: for instance eco-fascists. There is one side with power and the other side with impotence. I deal with components of a certain tradition. The Arc of Triumph as a tank. The old language of architecture was highly symbolic. It's hard to remain a pessimist. I deal with war and military rituals with irony; but what is the spectator seeing? Pacasmayo, Paranagua, Kingston, Trapezunt, en transito, in Kraftshof read the zinc stencils in his studio.

**

My taxi driver, from Eritrea, will not believe there is snow now, in May, in Scotland. That's the North Pole, he says. He asks if Scotland is part of the United Kingdom. Nor will he believe the police in Scotland do not routinely carry guns. He can't drop me off in front of the station, it's not allowed. The Bavarian Police are very strong, he says. It's the Feast of the Ascension, a holy day of obligation.

**

The elderly woman with the dog will not direct me to the Underground station, but instead takes my arm and leads me there. Her grey-muzzled dog pauses at every tree and each lamp-post. She pauses. There are other dog walkers at this early hour and she keeps her shambling dog on a short lead. You must take care with dogs, she says. If you have a dog you know lots of people. The dog sniffs at the base of a lime tree. I can't tell her I'm in a hurry. The sky is unclouded. The sun warms her, the old dog and me.

**

The Mayor, in his second term of office, tells me that politics on a local level has a special place in democracy: If I go to the market and buy vegetables the people speak to me.

**

The coffee maker, buyer and blender, discusses the origins of his coffee and the rules of how to make the best of his beans.
The Artist, in a red jacket, orange trousers, purple shoes and a lime tee shirt poses in front of his painting. It's a painting of his ex who was always late. I count the incorporation of sixty-six clocks.
The tee shirt maker was a graphic designer. She learned her transfer techniques from Japanese methods.
Outside the vintage shop the angel spits water unendingly into the fountain.
In their short avenue, Willie, Ellen and Elisabet each

tend an individual plane tree.
Shadows grow.

**

Herr Wolf, the butcher, arranges a cooking competition between the Mayor and a Conservative.

**

Small children skip across Spitalgasse. A man in green shoes spins a red ball.
Everywhere poplar seeds on air drift into shafts of sun.

**

The doorman has volunteered for Blaue Nacht. He is seventy one years old, yes. He has a son of fifty three. He only gave up football last year because of a shoulder injury. Now he takes part in the Senior Olympics, has been a finalist many times. The crowd becomes pressing and is sweeping me into the House of the Holy Ghost. Parting, we shake hands, thumbs clasped. Inside there is a tray of M&M packets and prosecco for guests.

**

Are you looking for the toilet? Come with me says a man inside the café on Bergstrasse. Where are you from he asks; and Excuse me, as he delicately breaks wind. Tell the Czech and Polish at your table this is unique.

**

Up late, the wee girl runs wide eyed. Mama! Mama! she says and her long white dress is clean against the blue skirt of her mother as she hugs her mother's legs, for the sheer love of childhood, of the late night, of spring and grown up voices all along the street.

**

To Trude's secret delight Bayern did not win the match against Chelsea.

**

Pia, at seven, knows it's the headlights of cars in the street two storeys down making the lit-up shapes of windows on the white ceiling, but she doesn't know how. The window patterns sweep left to right and right to left, growing longer as they reach the walls, where they disappear. The best, the slowest, are the ones from right to left. When it happens both ways together, it's too fast, like scuttling spiders. It's an enchantment each night that sends her to sleep. She might sleep for a hundred years.

**

He accepts the archaeology of his dreams, with the more recent at the top. Here and there, fault lines. Those old dreams below the surface fractured, broken, compressed.

**

Oh, and Olof forgot the clouds: cumulus, piling to the east beyond vision.

**

Hanne's fingers are long. They caress the mushrooms they are slicing with the wooden-handled knife.

**

The white pigeon pecks between the granite setts among the blown blossom under the Robinia trees in Hans Sachs Platz. The bird is not a symbol.

**

The Editor-in-Chief says this town has some ugly parts. He wanted to say this before. His dear old mother-in-law, who's eighty-five, sometimes forgets his name. At the editorial conference, body language and lack of eye contact tell a different, unreadable, story. The paper has sixty journalists who pray for the publisher every day.

**

The white pigeon flutters to the left as Arnold's expensive bike comes too close. The artist does not see the bird, one of many.

**

Effi did her Masters in Manchester, She says she's

just quit her job as a magazine journalist because she can't get on with her boss, whose partner in any case owns the magazine. She's fluent and damning in her appraisal of her boss. As a waiter, her other job in Hans Sachs Platz, she handles all orders with grace and humour.

**

The white pigeon is back, early.

**

The Historian says the beginning was in 1918. The elite could not accept defeat. Architecture was a symbol of intended world rule. The idea was to fill the arenas, the stadiums with thousands. The US Ambassador visited in 1938 and approved of this plan. That year, Adolf Hitler announced the intention to invade Czechoslovakia. The investigation into the past is to ensure such things can never happen again.

**

He sees the unfinished Nazi Congress Hall, intended to hold fifty thousand folk, slowly being reclaimed by trees and by Dürer's Great Lawn. Leaving the Hall, his unconscious leads him to hum Handel's aria from Judas Maccabaeus "See the conqu'ring hero come". Outside, the benches, in full sun, are built high. The women swing their legs like young girls.

**

The wall speaks: Nvllvm crimen, nvlla poena sine lege – kein Verbrechen, keine Strafe ohne Gesetz. No crime, no punishment, without law.

**

Angelika was young, a freelance journalist, just starting out. In 1985, she sat in the Press seat inside Nuremberg Court 600 for yet another Nazi trial of an insignificant but murderous Party member.

**

The white pigeon says a tree is a tree is a tree.

**

The Tavern Choir sings in the darkening garden behind Bucherstrasse.
There is a bottle for them each of white Franconian wine. A salad. The singing is spontaneous: they are four friends and have been at practice in the flat upstairs. They laugh and sing. The stars are in the sky above the rooftops. There is no audience. Bats flit above the trees.

**

The Thai woman lifts crates of drinks for the cafe two at a time from the boot of the car. She shifts one to her left hand, keeping one in her right and swings them both up the five sandstone steps to the back door of the café where she works. The sun is hot already. A bunch of keys swings from a long cord at her belt and bangs her knees. She does not pause at all, now bringing empty crates from inside the cafe to the car. A tram passes up the hill.

**

The white pigeon says: Albrecht, you never really look at birds. Take your engraving for the Apocalypse – where the angels have better wings than that odd eagle, who's saying ~bebebe – what's that? You know the one: in the Seven Trumpets in the Secret Revelation of St John – the Apocalypse at the End of Time. Have you never seen a dove feather flutter down from a lime tree?

**

Outside the Convent the nun has laid a table from which she sells Asterix comics. There is an honesty box.

**

Floods of fallen blossoms line the side streets.

**

The men sitting outside Franco's drinking coffee

and white wine at noon are getting on. Their hair is thinning, swept back. There are ear-rings, two tone shoes. As they leave, one or two at a time, they hitch up their trousers. Each one lights a cigarette. The world is still here.

Sweeney Albannach

I heard the cuckoo with no food in my stomach.
Malcolm MacLellan, Crofter, Grimnis, Benbecula
as reported in Carmina Gadelica

fragments 1 – 105

that fat spider hung
on translucence
then there was
only a great white
raggy winged moth
I catched it
in hand but felt
pity
then

**

the dog it was
found my place
in heather

**

you count these
no worth
buttercup daisy thistle
the quadrated plants
rare words I found
but did not pluck
you count these
ravings of invisibility
they know better

**

his head sits his body
only queerly

**

guilt tears
worse than blackthorn

**

goosegrass
but no geese

**

whisky oh
whisky oh
whisky in the bushes oh
thorns don't matter

**

and then we examine
the politics of our time
and find still
Church

**

the moral law
of birdsong

**

my poetry
is entirely made up
of the sounds of rain
on leaves

**

it's that form of silence
I call wandering
that form of wandering
you call delusion

**

you think me deranged
to return as oak
looking over the kyles
stand for a thousand years

**

the elder is in awe
the cuckoo agrees
the yaffle agrees
the gulls mock me

**

that night I wove the clouds

**

wild honey
bee stings
the flaying syrup
of self pity

**

Sweeney attempts to list all things
on the strand

**

seals and singing

**

Sweeney is not suffering
his head
the world is indifferent

**

once he found a case of oranges

**

have you known hunger
withered windfall
in May

**

Sweeney seen

deer slots on the strand

**

farewell to Lochaber
or maybe petrol city

**

only the cuckoo
calls hello
two gowks together
until night
drops

**

Sgurr nan Gillean
Ainshval
Askival
Hallival
just a view
hungry
something remembered
farmed out

**

I only wanted to lose
my name

**

loitering
outside the village
hall unbidden un
invited eaves
dropping gossip and come
hither talk
maybe someone will
drop a long dout
still lit

**

the cant
and antiphon
of shearwaters
a mouthful
of cress
to my ache

**

I sit here
counting puffins
inventing words

**

there are no mirrors

**

below the yellow hill there
are caves
that keep out the rain
but not the reaches of cold
nor the midges' perforations

**

rusty hinge
of a lapwing's
voice
and unhinged
me

**

I am beside myself
where the best conversations
are to be had

**

the fattest snails
are found
in the graveyard

**

I steal eggs from the gulls
and from Mary's hens
crack and swallow

**

when I pass
they knit their brows
along with
their children's socks
only Sweeney

dusty
is unspun

**

twelve by twelve inches
a square foot
what I'm here for
the first cast of the quadrat
one buttercup
one nettle
one stem of cleavers
I remain empty

**

show me the passage
between the poised mind
and the frenzied mind

**

where I live
you've not been

**

there's a high wind
in my lungs
to give life
to the fire

**

it's rude to sit
with your back
to the sun
every cormorant knows that

**

there's the black cat
who visits
each morning
to roll and have
her stomach scratched
she doesn't know I'm broken
and there's a toad
who
lives around the corner

**

I drink red wine
from the kettle
for this moment I
am Li Po
that same wind rattles
our watery retreats

**

the cuckoo sings
two notes
as she flies
indefatigable
how can I be less

**

the deserted church
browned flowers
broken gas mantles
heh. heh. priests
gone from this place
but still seclusion

**

stealing apples
while eras
and stars
collapse around me

**

although I am conceived and die
I conceive of yet more

**

the priests even
atheists
maunder words
of soul and spirit
blasphemies of belief
such things are in
slaters and wrens

**

fear me
cry me gealt
because you fear
change
you fear revolution

**

there is no rest
at night stars
Saturn distant Mars
cold Jupiter
in the church ruin
a Sheela na gig
I flee even her
mound of Venus

**

the tempest takes
hurls the dove
I run into the heart
there is no abiding there

**

when the rain lifts
tracing snail trails
on the rock
with a cold finger

**

at night I
waken to myself
not there
either

**

pouring water
another vertigo
to fall

**

plover fears me
flees on a path of air
clatter of dove wing

rising from oak
startles me to run
into the path of bramble
dread keeps us living

**

before the storm
the cuckoo's complaint
after the storm
cuckoo's lament
I'm still here too
after all

**

beside the rear
tractor wheel
its tyre flat
a stainless
steel socket set
and rusty headed hammer
crow on the cab roof
things are not
urgent

**

roof mostly sky
walls to east and south
sgurrs
north and west
seas
the robin hops inside
crows row through

**

iron tractor seat
rust and no backside
for years
I climb up
change rusty gears
make a child's
mouth noise driving
how happy I am
not to plough

**

chair's a rounded stone
doubtless some saint or other
thought it his

truth is he only borrowed it
passed on
I remain here

**

sing to the laverock
as she rises her song
clear liquid with
immanence
mine too

**

in the glen of sloes
on the hill of blueberries
at the burn with cress
wild garlic nettle soorocks
keeping still behind a trunk
when folk go by in hiking gear
chattering no one
sees Sweeney
self-exiled
nothing to say

**

walked three miles for
the two onions I saw yesterday
and forgot to pocket
haven't the tang of sorrel

**

you cook everything
I eat raw greens
mind begets mind

**

when I lost my pencil
I wrote with a sandstone pebble
on walls

**

the wildlife bus
is still on the jack
no chance of them
coming across me then

**

I was
not even she sheela na gig
looks at me with tenderness
or lust

**

seven swans
the only warmth I have
from the stings of nettles

**

O I was flyin
the jinkin hare

**

how close the turf is
how sweet the bluebells' scent
nesting down the night

**

sometimes it can take a long time
to find the right stone

**

thought I'd piss on the
beached bleached log
see how long it'd take
this wind to dry it

**

second throw of the quadrat
unknown grasses
must look them up
and a leafing ranunculus

**

third throw of the quadrat
of note forget-me-not
ribwort plantain silverweed

**

fourth throw of the quadrat
horsetail yellow iris for the poet
I also know as flags but despair

**

fifth throw of the quadrat
tormentil silverweed forget-me
-not

**

that bell of bluebell
hare of harebell
silver of silverweed
the torment of tormentil
the forget me of forget-me-not
the bitterness of bittercress

**

nails brittle and black
tiny pignuts washed in

the waterfall for supper
once I drank malt whisky

**

Sweeney's Way
rowan on a hillside
rooted into a glacial erratic
broken bluebell in the hole
of a limestone pebble

**

there are things
which flash past
peripheral vision
they will betray me

**

you are intemperate
he is intoxicated
with possibility

**

the hard mouth of the snipe
and the soft utterance of a lapwing

**

show me in your shops
where you can buy nettles
or soft May sunlight
as it edges to the sea
across heather and rush

**

how do I move from the past
to present but
by the astonishment of a peewit
how do I move from the
present to the past but
by the twitching throw
of a pebble as I sink
into sleep the way a seal
slips back into the waves

**

an old mongrel he
sometimes wriggles
with sheer joy
at the remembered name of a plant
oxytropis
then terror strikes
must run off past
Beinn Buidhe

**

lucid and ludic
is madness that whirl
of hair flying round
Sweeney's head
that tilt into wind
as he lifts his arms
and rolls earth words

**

fuck the polis
such lyricism is easy
fuck the priests
but they screw themselves

with faith and certitude
and there's only the last lit pale
constellations of ramsons here
on out into blue black
bruise starred night

**

the seventh throw of the quadrat
early purple orchid wild garlic
raspberry leaves bluebells
bracken red campion but outwith
the confines of the quadrat
they grow where they please

**

the eighth quadrat on rock
white lichen red lichen
these are not symbols
not the thing
not the opposing
conjoined forces
of church and state
but substantive

**

my love gave me a meadow
that walked to the sea
my love gave me every seventh wave
that licked gently
my love gave me the seven days
and I am Sweeney
called mad

**

the young birch in wind
a child approaching

**

in search of fossils
found in that future
three speckled eggs
in the oystercatcher's nest

**

that which resolves itself in sleep
is lost to Sweeney

**

yes I'm scared jittery
twitching jumping
alert mistrustful
but I haven't fear
living in me

**

where do my eyes lead me
what I see I am
clinging bramble vine
raking thorn peat hag
and cuckoo voice
invisible

**

overseer of wind
narrator of air
conductor of skies
moonhandler
star-juggler
sun-lifter
breath of your lungs
without memory
continuous

**

move steeply
into that rising
scree-slope night
collapsing on itself
that hides

**

Sweeney
startled
startles
a snipe

**

Sweeney's clarity is inside
may be illuminated
briefly by a quality of
light pushing
cloud shadows
lighting gullies and cliffs in a chequered
way
on a three mile distant mountain

**

their taste in whisky was poor

**

Armeria maritime
thrift
we call it
Sweeney has nothing
no need for thrift
stays nights
here and there in old small
rail cabins
Rannoch Corpach Arisaig
some have full roofs

**

I no longer need to know
who I am
indeed and I don't
my voice
embodied

**

aspen
Sweeney
by Ardtoe slip
tremble
in each
breeze

**

green
beyond green

on being in a place / on being in place

(A nine day walk across Scotland)

Hedderwick

we could have planted
an oar here
but we stitched
the land
a palimpsest
an ecology of utterance
place of heather

Houston Mill

a broken willow branch
& her blue eyes
walk with us
our time collapsed
our vanities
the Way
a route from here to there

Craigmoor

visions of a land
denuded of history
leaving only parted lips
a gone song
for miners
for shepherds
pollen for bees

Cregg's Wood

what's the manifest
of timber
leaves and light
what's manifest
in timber
cruck and book
and cradle   cradle

Peffer Bank

perhaps
in irony
honesty
seeds itself
at the gate
of the
Big House

North Woods

this is the way of it
war after war
deer scut
northern woods
grow slowly
round coastal concrete
defence blocks

Castle Garden of Water Beyond

the night sky
is studded
women are singing
a last song stolen from time
what is the ground
of making
of proving

Dalmeny, Long Green

and slow
the slow of millennia
move to this
this slow
immediate
and immediately
passed

Wester Shore Wood

north sea walking
the littoral
moon pulled
acid blue
plastic rainbow
gull hull
model submitted

Viaduct

the eye's
reverie and rest
each limb
of each tree
underlit in
evening in
luminous energy

Gilston

right there
a high wind
hover folds
herself to earth
a vole is pierced
nothing
is claimed

Kelvinhead

when lucidity fails
the green leaf
becomes brown
the brown leaf
becomes blown
down
earth as one

Bar Hill

the stride
is longer
in the long grass
we ride the world
we tumble it
with our tread
caress of our feet

Shirva

all the west
moves west
languages seed
and migrate
vowels stretch
here is a beginning
the curlew sings

Balglas

the rhythm of moor
is determined by stones
the language is of tongues
in solitude
tones emerge
one walk
becomes another

Finglen Burn

this spider fishes
in pelagic air
for small fleeting lives
little bear or dog
swan and crab
bull under lion
who fishes for stars

Standing Stones

a letter to a lover
of exile's shadow
or shadow's unlifting
of the long sorrow of land
of the cuckoo
of how love
survives if we can

Dumgoyach

nothing is broken
a buzzard mewls
there are winds
treeline covers
the summit
sky softly
laverock

Conachra

a collection of folds
cumulus cloud
gorse billow
sheep fank
fazed brain
of it all
time folded

Blairbeich

as if there were
boundaries between
breast and breast
between where the deer
lies and the deer
lying in this field
and the fallen

Ledrishbeg

the small thorns
catch us
each one impales
memory
we arrive and depart
as if that were
possible

Bannachra Woods
such kin
these woods
relatives to grow us
in glades in groves
dappled
mythic   logic
erotic

Blackhill Plantation

walls of black-
bird calls
thickened light
leaf light leaf
filtered
dwell a
while

.

Acknowledgements

Some of these poems were first published in the following journals: Reliquiae, Earthlines, Writers Magazine China, sma buiks, Gutter and Levure littéraire, with Spanish translations in Prometeo
    Some excerpts from Sweeney Albannach were published as an ebook by otata's bookshelf.
    Island Stories first appeared in the anthology You Don't Look British.
    A Brief Incomplete History of Nuremberg was made possible by a Hermann Kesten Stipendium.
    on being in a place was written during the inaugural walk of the John Muir Way while planting tree seeds with Andrew Schelling.

My thanks, as ever, to Morven Gregor for sage advice and great patience.